My Brother Evan

Written and Illustrated By Ashlyn Southard

DEDICATION

I dedicate this book to people who strive daily to make our world more inclusive.

FORWARD

Ashlyn wrote this book about her brother, Evan, when she was in kindergarten. One day I asked her if she knew what Fragile X Syndrome was and she said yes. I asked her if she would like to wrote a story about our family and the following book was dictated to me.

Our family has since grown! We have been blessed with the additions of Benjamin (2008), Clare (2010), Gianna (2012), Ava (2015), and Joshua (2014). My children make me so proud. Each is a gift and wonderful in his or her own unique way. They each hold an amazing sensitivity and deep sibling love for each other. God has blessed me with them and their wonderful Dad, Scott.

I am forever grateful.

Diane Southard (Mom)

My name is Ashlyn. I have a brother and a sister and a mom and a dad. I have a pet bird. My bird's name is Birdie because I couldn't decide what to name him.

My brother has Fragile X Syndrome. That is something when people don't learn as quick as other people. Maybe it takes them longer to walk and talk. I am patient with him. He has therapy to help him learn things faster.

Evan can say baby and movie. He likes T.V. He has

a special swing inside. It helps make him happier

when he is kind of grumpy.

I can help him jump on the trampoline by jumping on it. He likes to chase me. I still love him. My favorite thing to do with my brother is snuggle because it means he loves me.

My brother is three. He can walk and talk a little bit. I think he is having fun at preschool. He is my only bestest brother. Our little sister Cailey is funny. I go lots of places with my family, like the Magic House or the Zoo or California. I love my family. A true story.

Do you have a sibling with a disability?

Sometimes I feel left out of things that only Evan gets to

do. He gets to go to occupational and speech therapy.

He gets to play fun games and go on cool equipment. I

am not always allowed to join, that makes me kind of sad.

When I feel left out, I remember that his special

activities help him play, talk, and do activities by himself!

Is there anything that your sibling gets to do that you don't get to do?

Write a few ideas down!

_____

_____

_____

To help me feel included with Evan, I come up with fun things we can do together!

Evan and I...

Play outside together!

Watch our favorite movie together!

Make chocolate chip cookies!

What can you and your sibling do together?

Write a few ideas down!

_____

_____

_____

Fragile X Syndrome Facts

❖ Fragile X Syndrome (FXS) is something you are born with

❖ You cannot catch FXS from someone or develop it if you have never had it before

❖ About 1 in 4,000 people has FXS, that means about 100,000 American have FXS. That is about the same amount of people that visit Disneyland in one day.

❖ Kids with FXS often learn to walk, talk and do other things later than other kids.

❖ Calming activities such as swinging or rocking in a chair may help a child with FXS calm down if they become too excited. These are called sensory breaks.

❖ Kids with FXS often need extra help in school.

What we Know!

❖ Individuals with Fragile X Syndrome have fun, loving personalities and like to make other people happy.

❖ Kids with FXS like to do the same things as other kids. Most importantly all kids like to be included. Remembering to be patient, including a schedule and some sensory breaks can help make going someplace a great memory for everyone.

❖ Every person is capable of extraordinary things. Believe in others and support them to be the best they can be!

❖ One thing you can say to all kids is, "Hi!

Ashlyn and Evan Then (2005)

And Now (2017)

Our Family Now (2020)

The End

Discussion Questions

1. Do you know anyone with a disability?

2. How can you include EVERYONE in something you like to do?

3. What are different ways that you can say "Hi" to someone who doesn't use spoken language to communicate?

www.ingramcontent.com/pod-product-compliance
Lightning Source LLC
Chambersburg PA
CBHW060823290526
45792CB00005BB/1777